Sunny Fields

ISBN-10: 1717105025

ISBN-13: 978-1717105028

Color The Picture

Write Your Own Story

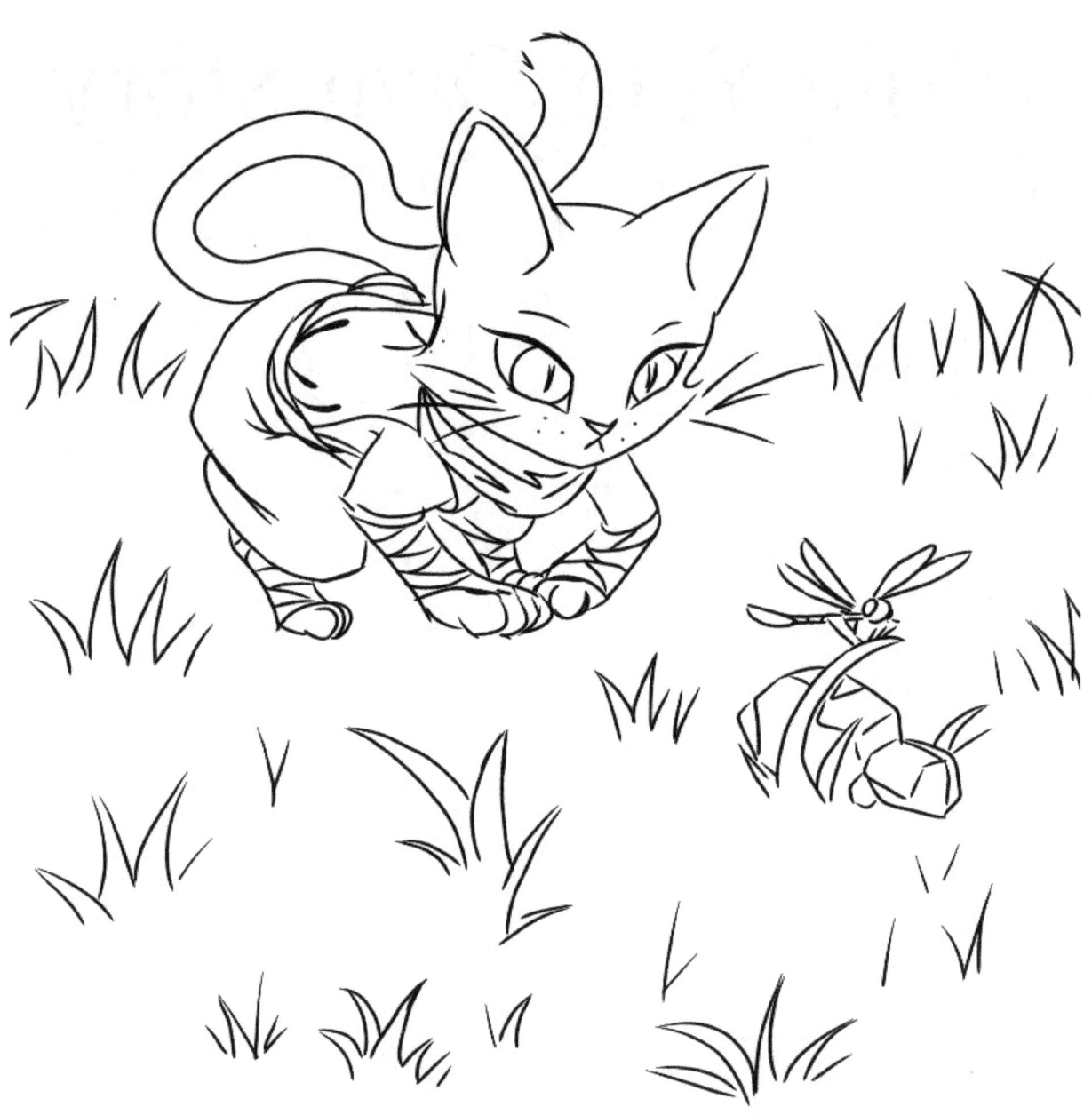

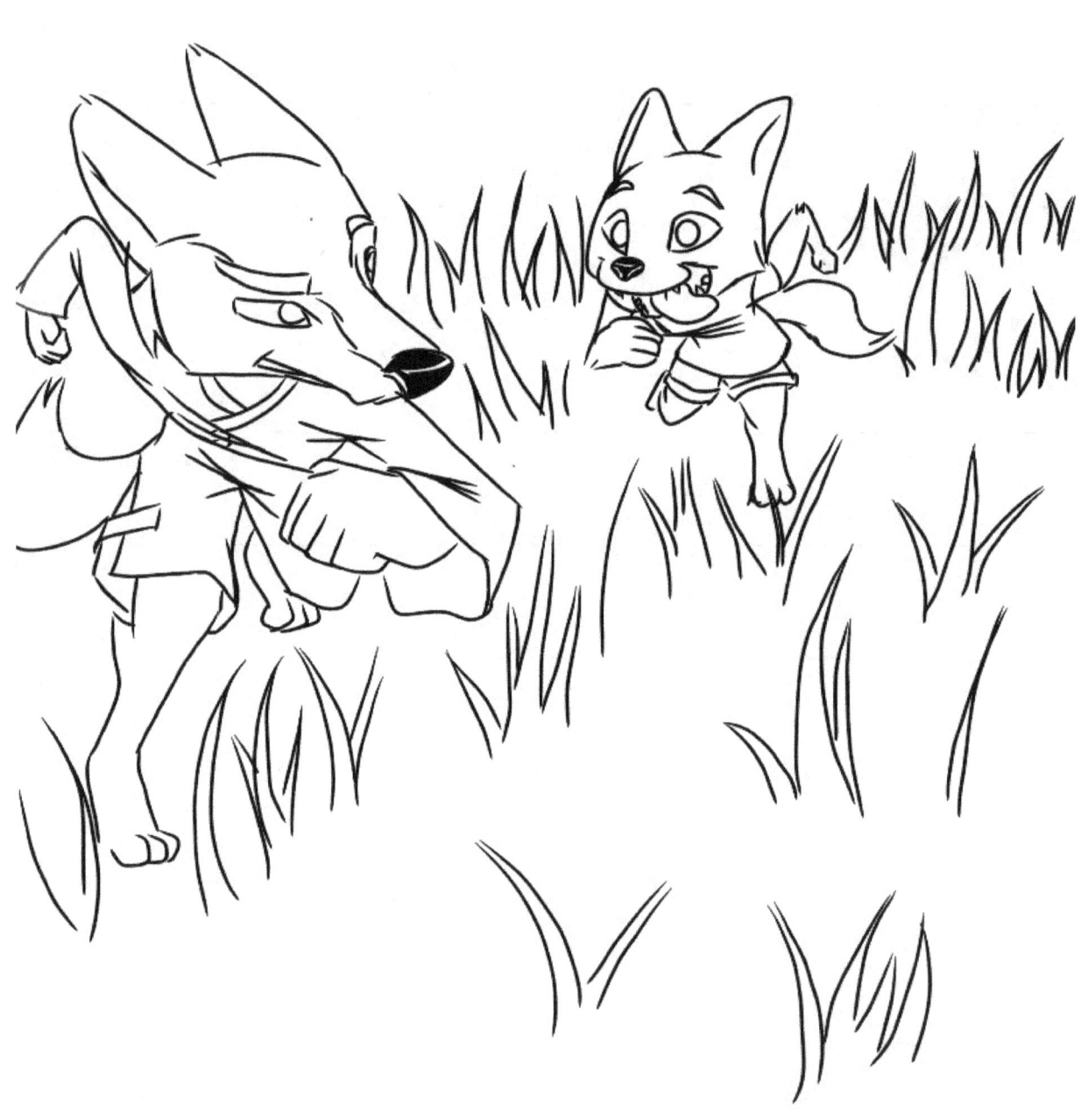

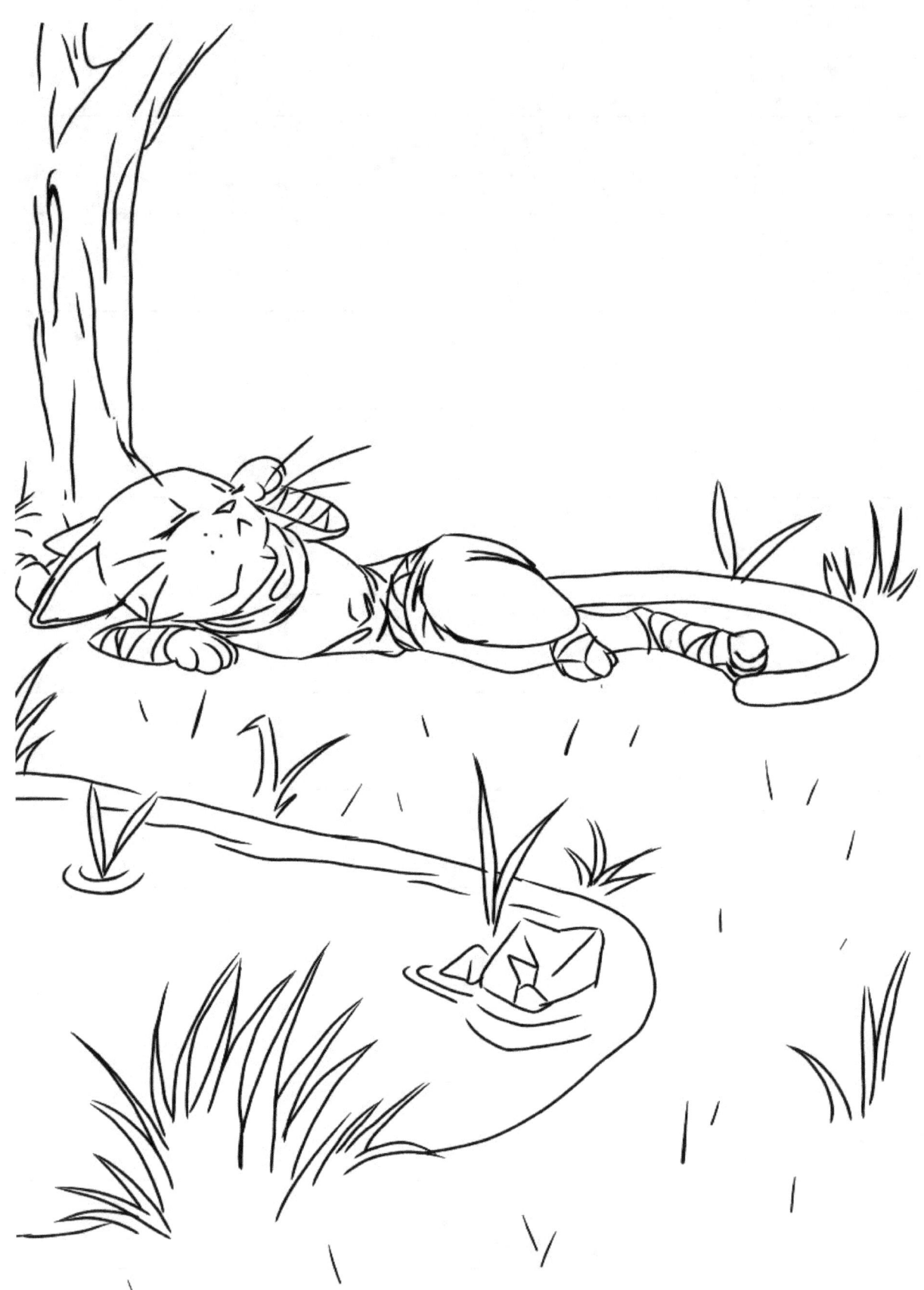

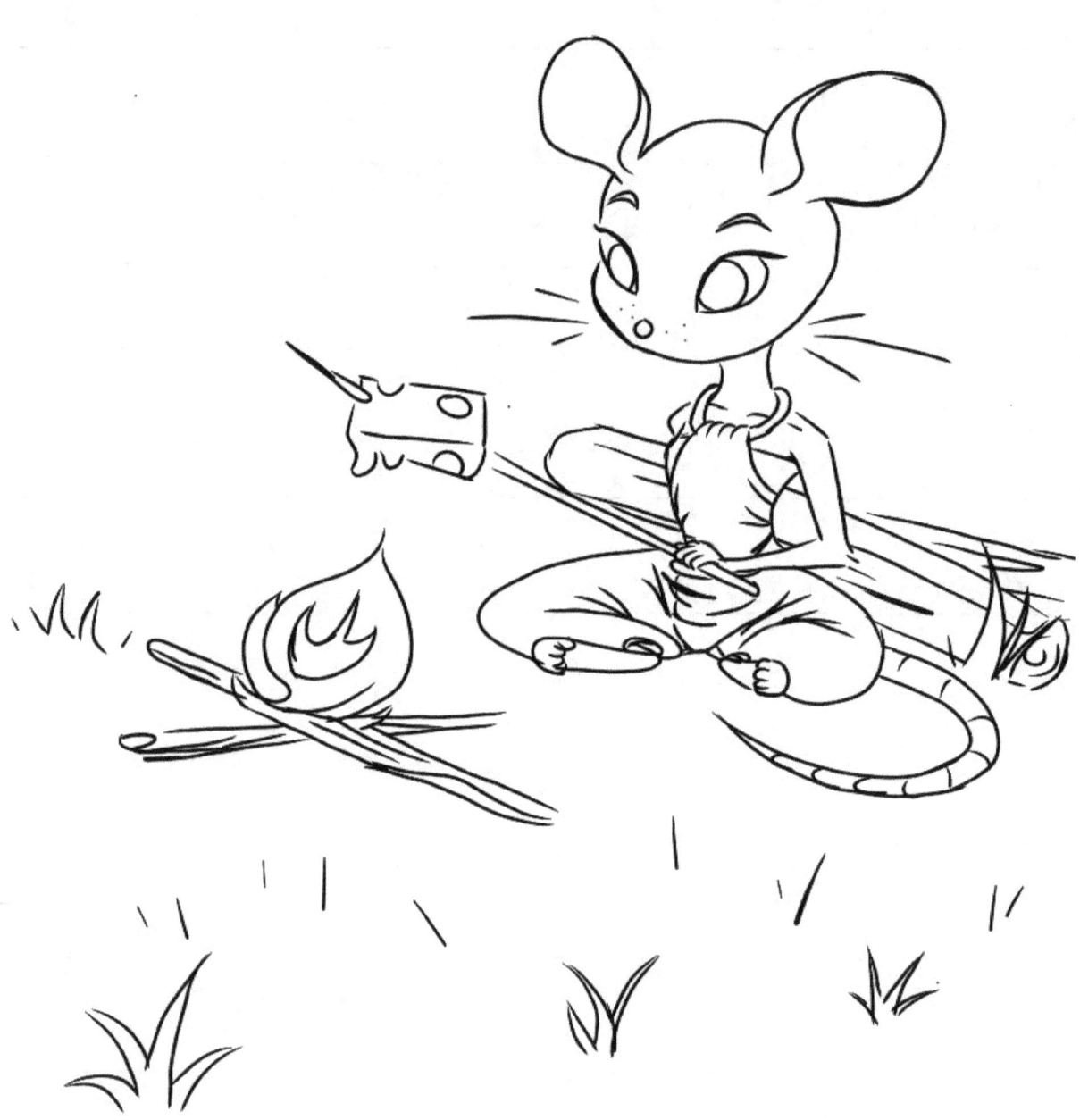

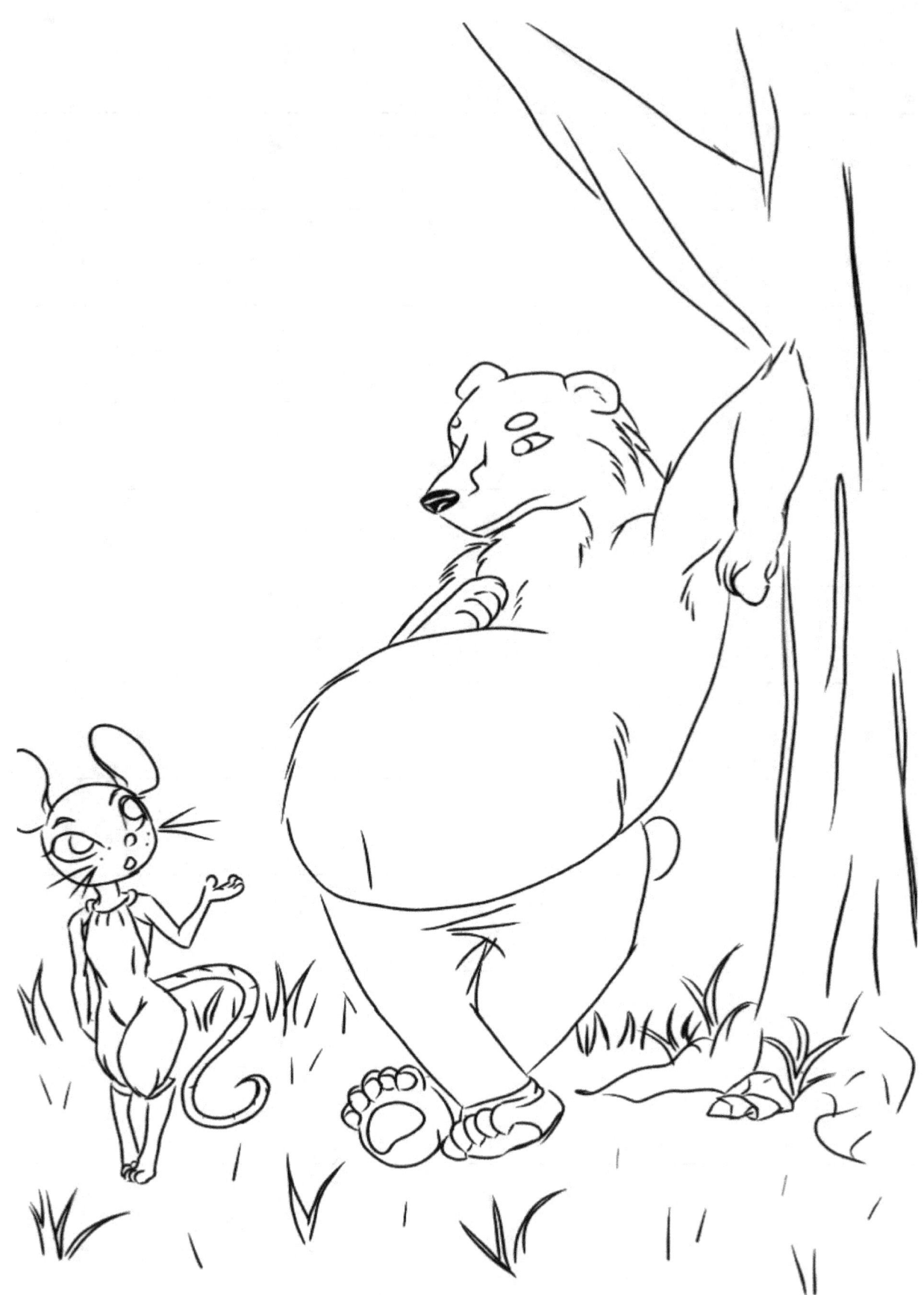

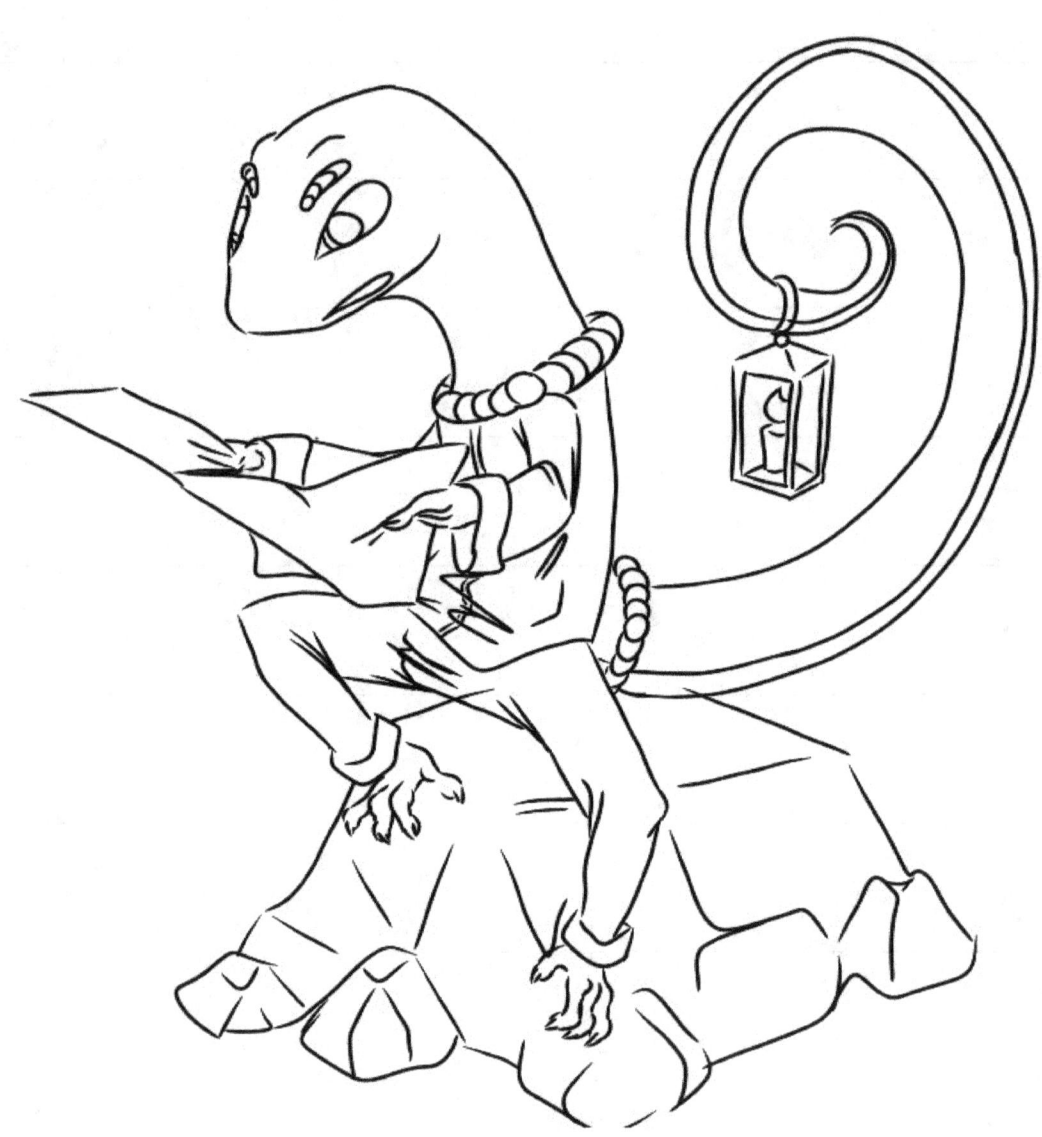

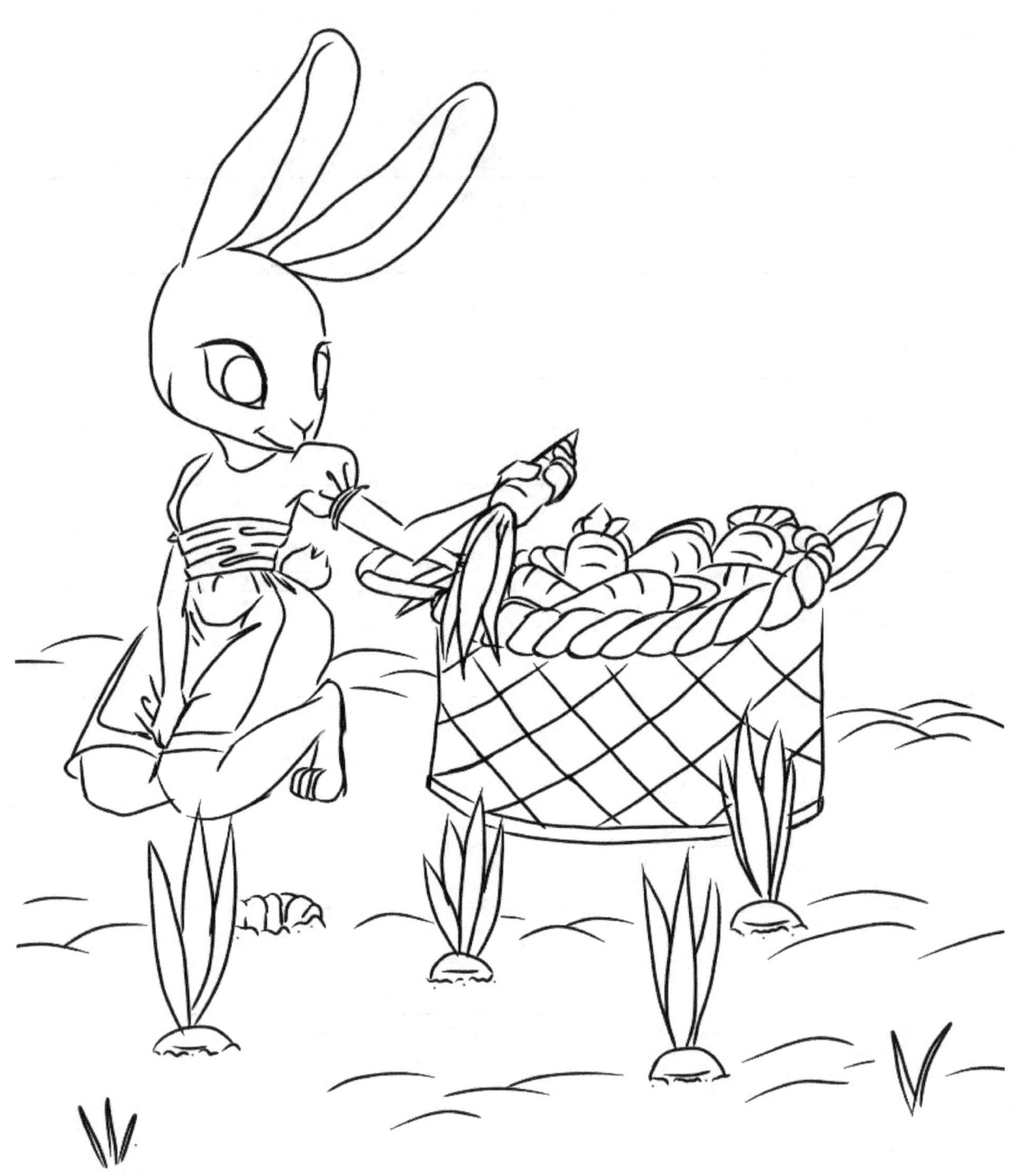

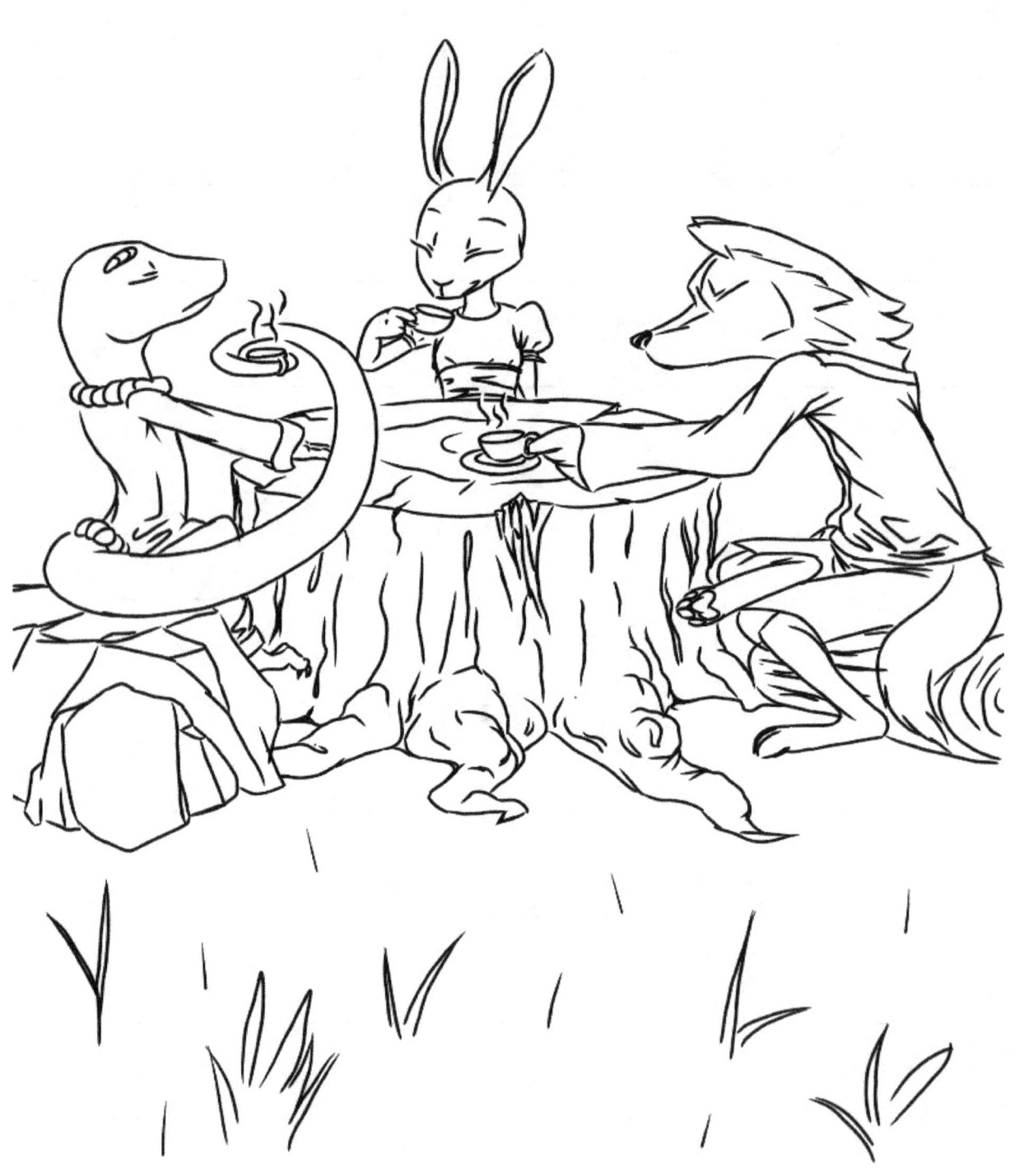

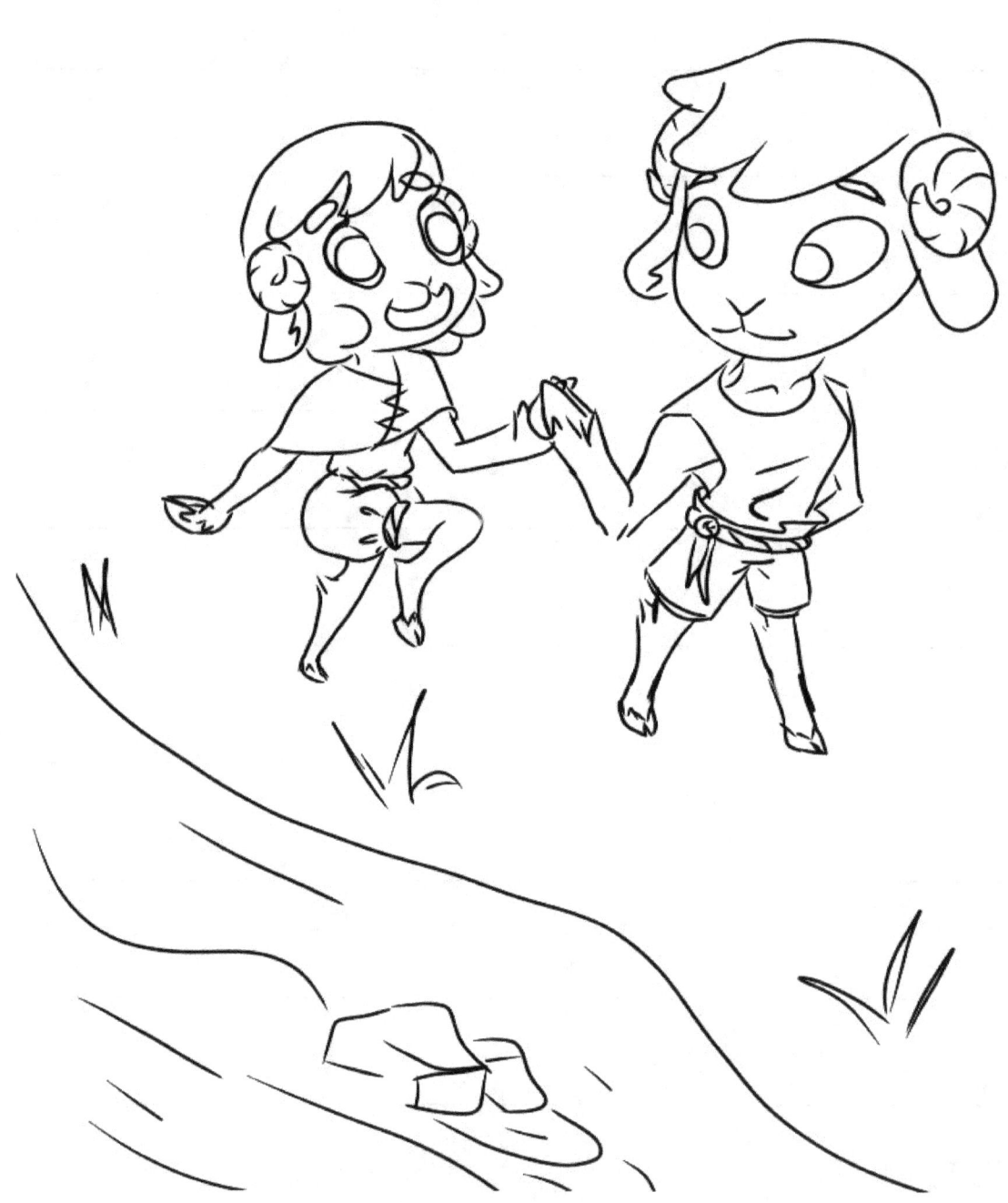

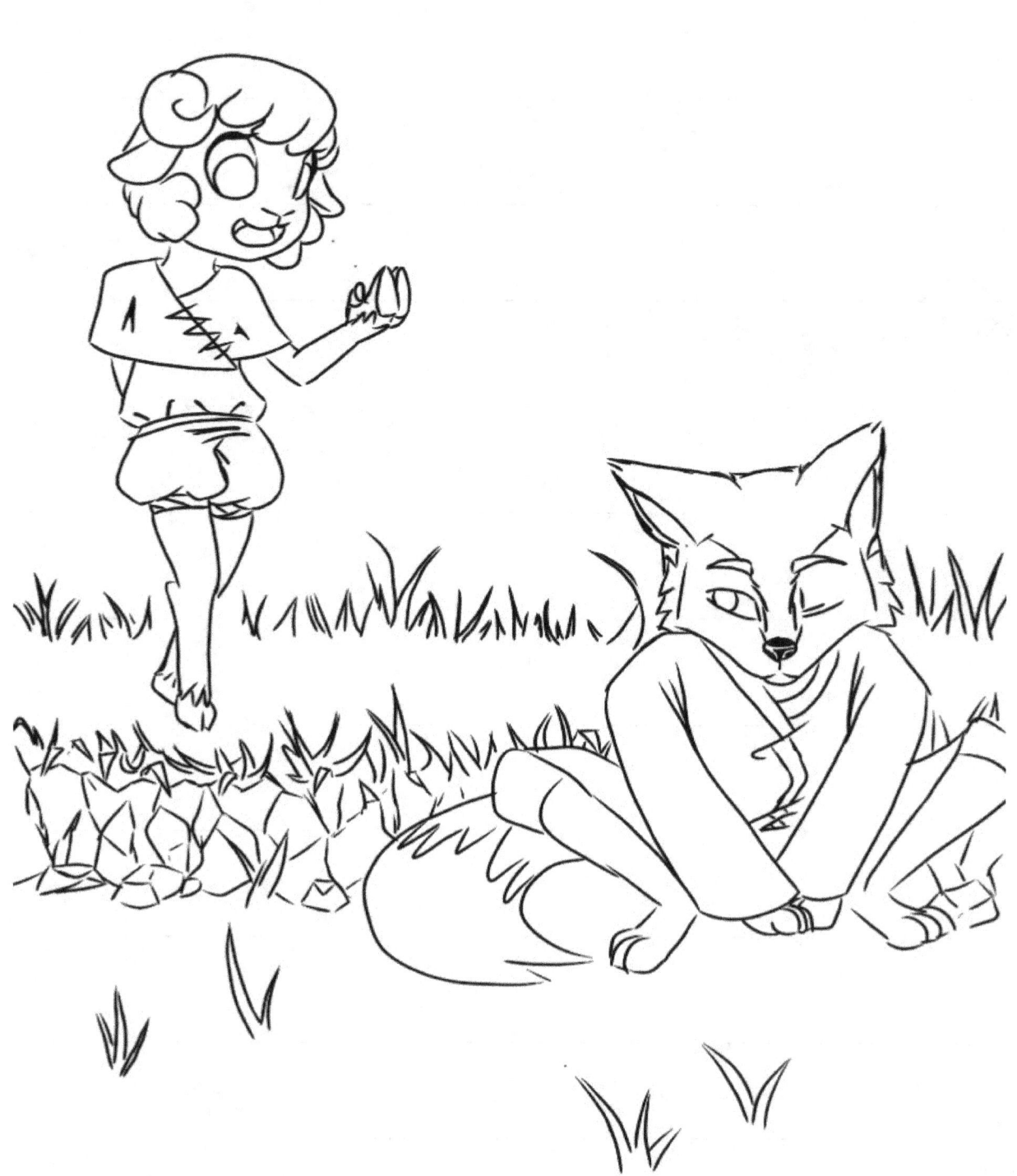

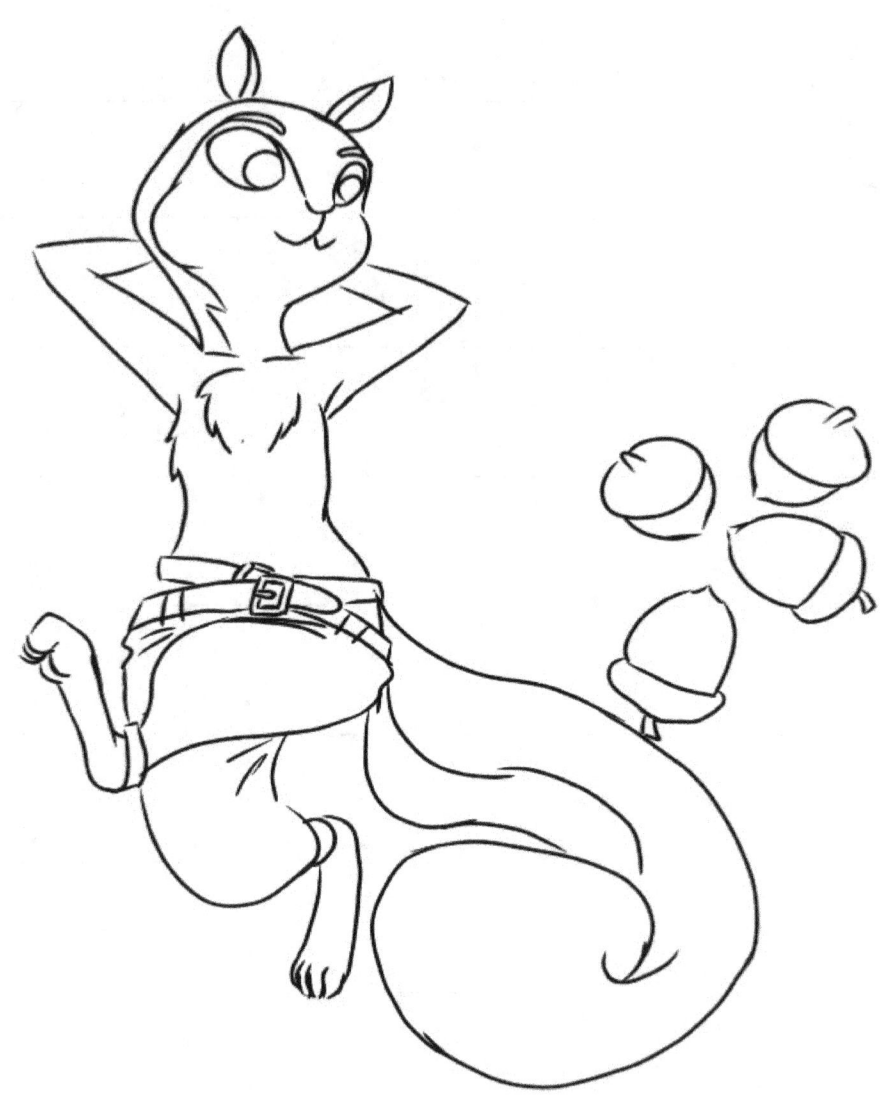

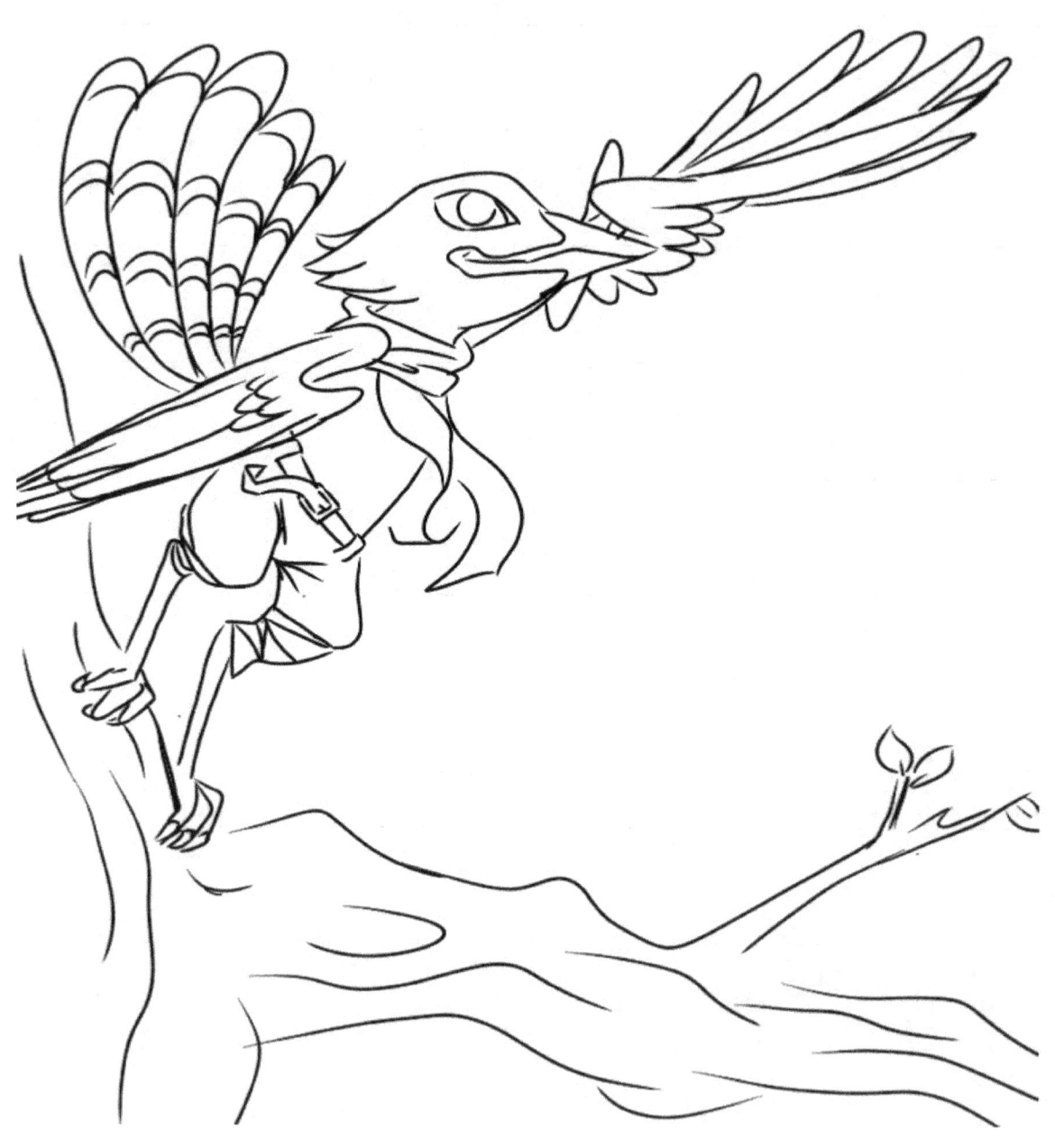

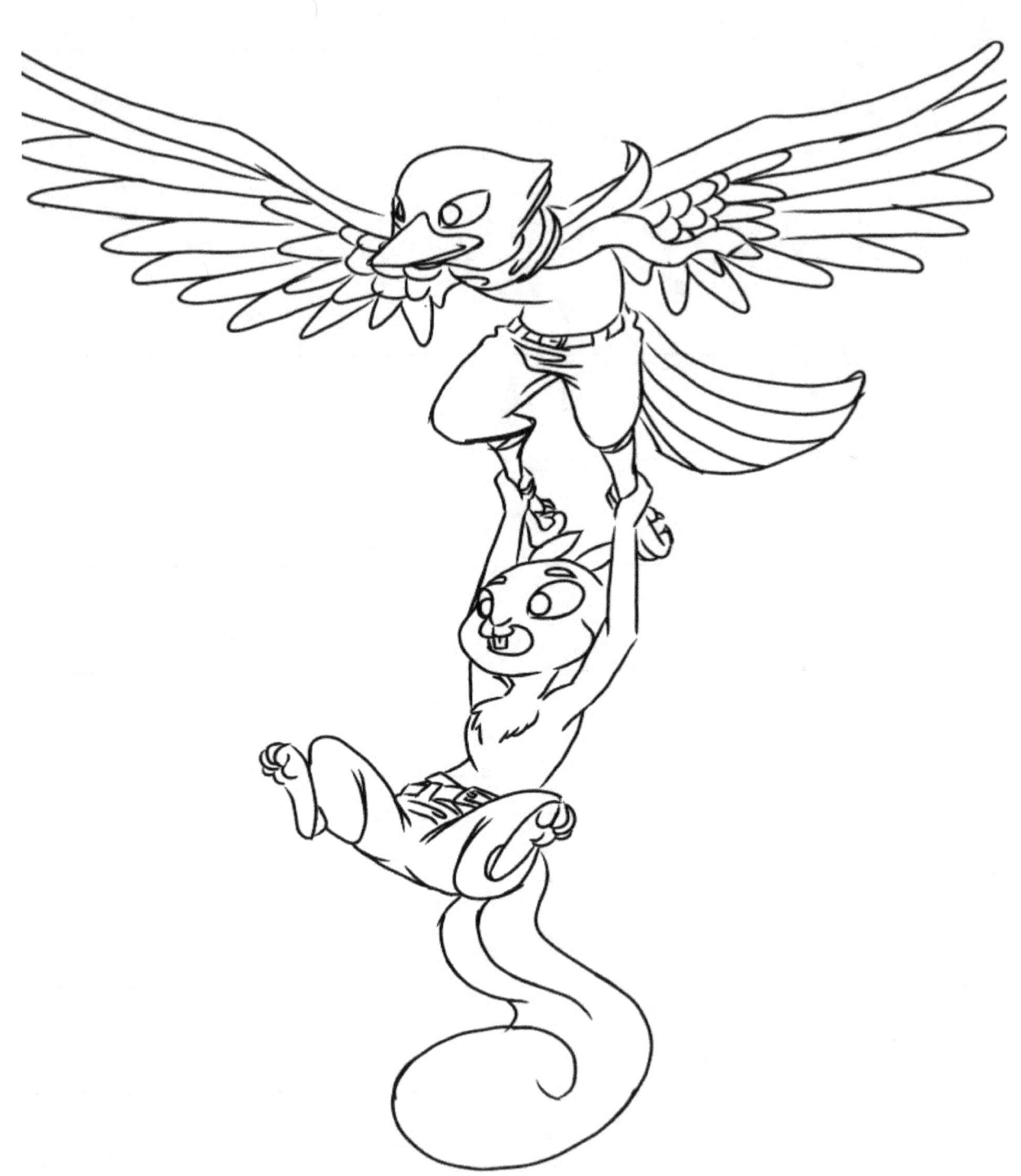

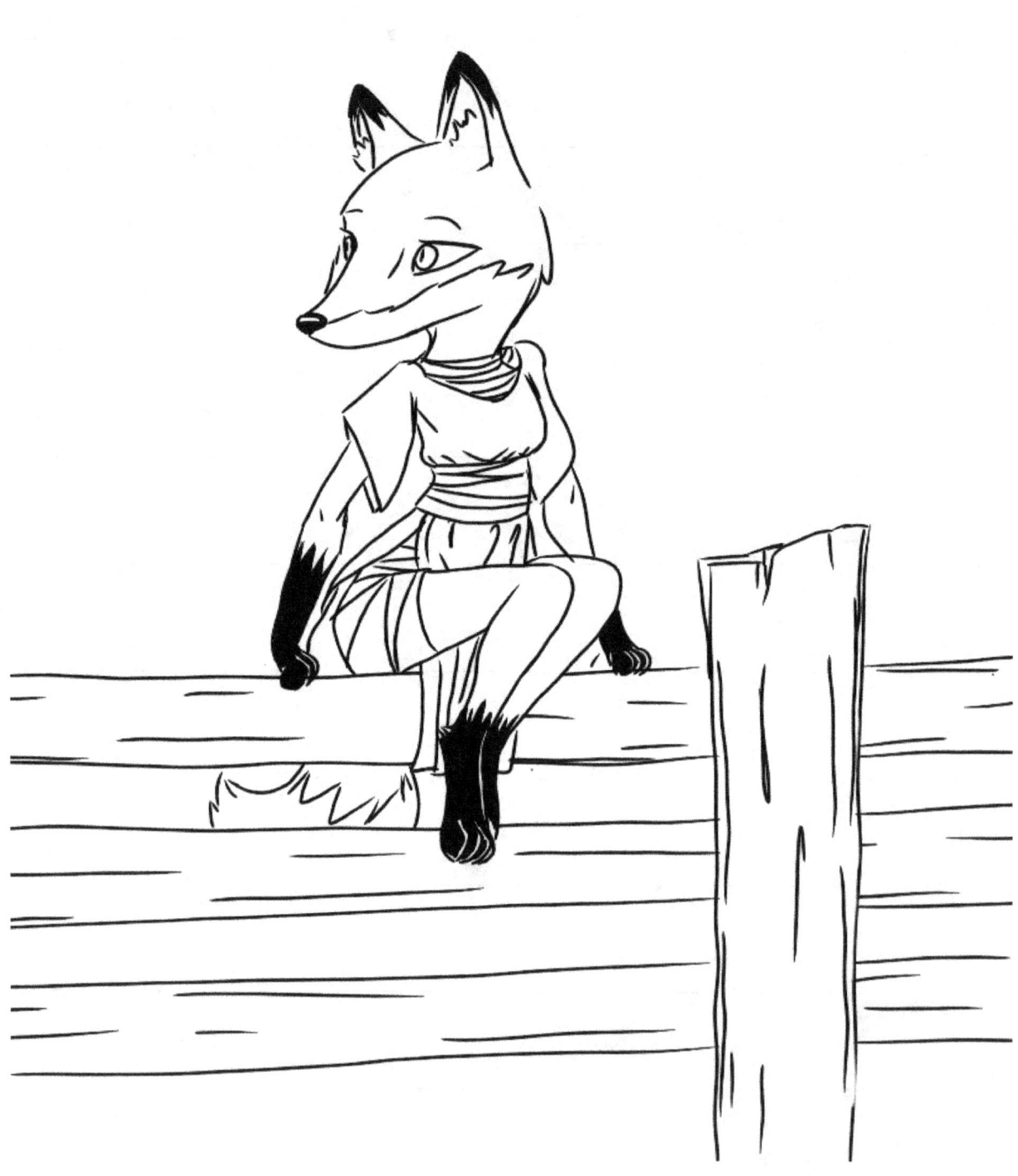

www.ingramcontent.com/pod-product-compliance
Lightning Source LLC
Chambersburg PA
CBHW081711220526
45467CB00019B/2782